KINGFISHER
a Houghton Mifflin Company imprint
222 Berkeley Street
Boston, Massachusetts 02116
www.houghtonmifflinbooks.com

First published in 1995 as *Who's There?*
This edition published in 2004
4 6 8 10 9 7 5 3

LIBRARY OF CONGRESS CATALOGING–IN–PUBLICATION DATA
Archibold, Tim.
Knock, Knock!/Tim Archibold—1st American ed.
p. cm.
1. Knock-knock jokes. 2. Wit and humor, Juvenile. I. Title.
PN6231.K55A73 1995
818'.5402—dc20 94-37193 CIP AC

ISBN 0-7534-5707-5

Printed in Canada
3TR/0704/TCL/HBM(PICA)/P400/C

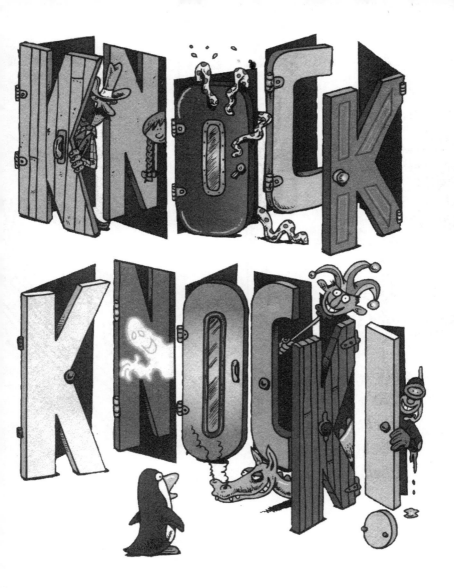

KNOCK KNOCK

The Best Knock Knock Jokes Ever!

KINGFISHER
BOSTON

KNOCK KNOCK!
Who's there?
Police.
Police who?
Police open up the door.

KNOCK KNOCK!
Who's there?
Isabelle.
Isabelle who?
Isabelle necessary on a bicycle?

KNOCK KNOCK!
Who's there?
Luke.
Luke who?
Luke through the keyhole and you'll see.

KNOCK KNOCK!
Who's there?
Ya.
Ya who?
I didn't know you were a cowboy!

KNOCK KNOCK!
Who's there?
Mr.
Mr. who?
Missed her at the bus stop.

KNOCK KNOCK!
Who's there?
Boo!
Boo who?
Don't cry, it's only a joke.

KNOCK KNOCK!
Who's there?
Atch.
Atch who?
Sorry, I didn't know you had a cold.

KNOCK KNOCK!
Who's there?
Micky.
Micky who?
Micky is lost so that's why I'm knocking.

KNOCK KNOCK!
Who's there?
Cereal.
Cereal who?
Cereal pleasure to meet you.

KNOCK KNOCK!
Who's there?
Alligator.
Alligator who?
Alligator toadstool but thought it was a mushroom.

KNOCK KNOCK!
Who's there?
Lettuce.
Lettuce who?
Lettuce in and we'll tell you.

KNOCK KNOCK!
Who's there?
Ivor.
Ivor who?
*Ivor a good mind not to
tell you.*

KNOCK KNOCK!

Who's there?
Alec.
Alec who?
Alec my lollipop.

KNOCK KNOCK!

Who's there?
Egbert.
Egbert who?
Egbert no bacon.

KNOCK KNOCK!

Who's there?
Colin.
Colin who?
Colin the doctor, I'm sick.

KNOCK KNOCK!
Who's there?
Sid.
Sid who?
Sid down and
have a cup of coffee.

KNOCK KNOCK!
Who's there?
Teresa.
Teresa who?
Teresa green.

KNOCK KNOCK!
Who's there?
Noah.
Noah who?
Noah don't know who you are either.

KNOCK KNOCK!
Who's there?
Justin.
Justin who?
Justin time for the party!

KNOCK KNOCK!
Who's there?
Banana.
Banana who?
KNOCK KNOCK!
Who's there?
Banana.
Banana who?
KNOCK KNOCK!
Who's there?
Orange.
Orange who?
*Orange you glad I
didn't say banana?*

KNOCK KNOCK!
Who's there?
Ken.
Ken who?
Ken I come in or do I have
to climb
through the
window?

KNOCK KNOCK!
Who's there?
Rover Seton.
Rover Seton who?
Rover Seton all my dinner and I'm starving!

Will you remember me tomorrow?
Yes.
Will you remember me in a week?
Yes.
Will you remember me in a month?
Yes.
Will you remember me in a year?
Yes.
KNOCK KNOCK!
Who's there?
Forgotten me already?

KNOCK KNOCK!
Who's there?
Major.
Major who?
Major answer didn't I?

KNOCK KNOCK!

Who's there?

Howard.

Howard who?

Howard you like to be outside for a change?

KNOCK KNOCK!
Who's there?
Senior.
Senior who?
Senior so nosy, I'm not going to tell you.

KNOCK KNOCK!
Who's there?
Wilma.
Wilma who?
Wilma lunch be ready soon?

KNOCK KNOCK!
Who's there?
Isaac.
Isaac who?
Isaac coming in!

KNOCK KNOCK!
Who's there?
Alfred.
Alfred who?
Alfred the needle if you sew.

KNOCK KNOCK!
Who's there?
Ammonia.
Ammonia who?
Ammonia little kid.

KNOCK KNOCK!
Who's there?
Amos.
Amos who?
Amos-quito bit me.

KNOCK KNOCK!
Who's there?
Andy.
Andy who?
Andy bit me again.

KNOCK KNOCK!
Who's there?
Anna.
Anna who?
Anna-ther mosquito!

KNOCK KNOCK!
Who's there?
Tennis.
Tennis who?
Tennis five plus five.

KNOCK KNOCK!
Who's there?
Cash.
Cash who?
I knew you were nuts.

KNOCK KNOCK!
Who's there?
Felix.
Felix who?
Felix my ice cream, I'll lick his.

KNOCK KNOCK!
Who's there?
Fletcher.
Fletcher who?
Fletcher self go!

KNOCK KNOCK!
Who's there?
Arthur.
Arthur who?
Arthur any more cookies in the jar?

KNOCK KNOCK!
Who's there?
Cynthia.
Cynthia who?
Cynthia been away, I've missed you.

KNOCK KNOCK!
Who's there?
Viola.
Viola who?
Viola sudden you don't know me?

KNOCK KNOCK!
Who's there?
Irma.
Irma who?
Irma big girl now.

KNOCK KNOCK!
Who's there?
William.
William who?
Williamind your own business.

KNOCK KNOCK!
Who's there?
Weirdo.
Weirdo who?
Weirdo you think you're going?

KNOCK KNOCK!
Who's there?
Handsome.
Handsome who?
Handsome spaghetti through the keyhole and
I'll tell you.

KNOCK KNOCK!
Who's there?
Nana.
Nana who?
Nana your business.

KNOCK KNOCK!
Who's there?
Yvonne.
Yvonne who?
Yvonne to be alone!

KNOCK KNOCK!
Who's there?
Alison.
Alison who?
Alison to my radio.

KNOCK KNOCK!
Who's there?
Scott.
Scott who?
Scott nothing to do with you.

KNOCK KNOCK!

Who's there?

Irish stew.

Irish stew who?

Irish stew in the name of the law!

KNOCK KNOCK!
Who's there?
Lena.
Lena who?
Lena little closer and I'll tell you.

KNOCK KNOCK!
Who's there?
Cows.
Cows who?
Cows go moo not who.

KNOCK KNOCK!
Who's there?
Europe.
Europe who?
Europe to no good.

KNOCK KNOCK!
Who's there?
Myth.
Myth who?
Myth you too.

KNOCK KNOCK!
Who's there?
Rabbit.
Rabbit who?
Rabbit up neatly. It's a present.

KNOCK KNOCK!
Who's there?
A little old lady.
A little old lady who?
I didn't know you could yodel.

KNOCK KNOCK!
Who's there?
Lionel.
Lionel who?
Lionel get you nowhere.

KNOCK KNOCK!
Who's there?
Jester.
Jester who?
Jester minute,
I'm trying to
find my key.

KNOCK KNOCK!
Who's there?
Snow.
Snow who?
Snow use, I've forgotten my key again.

KNOCK KNOCK!
Who's there?
Adelia.
Adelia who?
Adelia the cards and we'll play poker.

KNOCK KNOCK!
Who's there?
Eva.
Eva who?
Eva you're deaf or your doorbell isn't working.

KNOCK KNOCK!
Who's there?
Phyllis.
Phyllis who?
Phyllis in on the news.

KNOCK KNOCK!
Who's there?
Oscar.
Oscar who?
Oscar silly question, get a silly answer.

KNOCK KNOCK!
Who's there?
Francis.
Francis who?
Francis on the other side of the Atlantic.

KNOCK KNOCK!
Who's there?
Dimitri.
Dimitri who?
Dimitri is where lamb chops grow.

KNOCK KNOCK!
Who's there?
Scold.
Scold who?
Scold outside.

KNOCK KNOCK!
Who's there?
Jamaica.
Jamaica who?
Jamaica mistake?

KNOCK KNOCK!
Who's there?
Leaf.
Leaf who?
Leaf me alone!

KNOCK KNOCK!
Who's there?
Turnip.
Turnip who?
*Turnip the heat,
it's cold in here.*

KNOCK KNOCK!
Who's there?
Warrior.
Warrior who?
Warrior been all my life?

KNOCK KNOCK!
Who's there?
Midas.
Midas who?
Midas well open the door.

KNOCK KNOCK!
Who's there?
Theodore.
Theodore who?
Theodore is shut, please open it!

KNOCK KNOCK!
Who's there?
Olivia.
Olivia who?
Olivia but I've lost my key.

KNOCK KNOCK!
Who's there?
Gladys.
Gladys who?
Gladys Saturday, aren't you?

KNOCK KNOCK!
Who's there?
Robin.
Robin who?

Robin your house . . .

KNOCK KNOCK!
Who's there?
Stu.
Stu who?
Stu late to ask questions.

KNOCK KNOCK!
Who's there?
Wheelbarrow.
Wheelbarrow who?
Wheelbarrow some
money and go to Mexico!

KNOCK KNOCK!
Who's there?
Miniature.
Miniature who?
Miniature open the door, I'll tell you.

KNOCK KNOCK!
Who's there?
Congo.
Congo who?
Congo on meeting like this.

KNOCK KNOCK!
Who's there?
Jaws.
Jaws who?
Jaws truly.

KNOCK KNOCK!
Who's there?
Pasture.
Pasture who?
Pasture bedtime, isn't it?

KNOCK KNOCK!
Who's there?
Sherwood.
Sherwood who?
Sherwood like to come in, please.

KNOCK KNOCK!
Who's there?
Aardvark.
Aardvark who?
Aardvark a hundred miles
for just one of your smiles.

KNOCK KNOCK!
Who's there?
Iguana.
Iguana who?
Iguana hold your hand...

KNOCK KNOCK!
Who's there?
Doris.
Doris who?
Doris slammed on my finger. Ouch!

KNOCK KNOCK!
Who's there?
Tuna.
Tuna who?
Tuna your banjo and you can be in our band.

KNOCK KNOCK!
Who's there?
Moose.
Moose who?
Moose you be so nosy?

KNOCK KNOCK!
Who's there?
Gorilla.
Gorilla who?
Gorilla cheese
for me, please.

KNOCK KNOCK!
Who's there?
Stopwatch.
Stopwatch who?
Stopwatch you're doing right now!

KNOCK KNOCK!
Who's there?
Doughnut.
Doughnut who?
Doughnut open until Christmas.

KNOCK KNOCK!
Who's there?
Emma.
Emma who?
Emma bit cold out here, can you let me in?

KNOCK KNOCK!
Who's there?
Tyrone.
Tyrone who?
Tyrone shoelaces.

KNOCK KNOCK!
Who's there?
Stan.
Stan who?
Stan back or I'll shoot.

KNOCK KNOCK!
Who's there?
Nuisance.
Nuisance who?
What's nuisance yesterday?

KNOCK KNOCK!
Who's there?
Tuna.
Tuna who?
Tuna piano and it'll sound better.

KNOCK KNOCK!
Who's there?
Alli.
Alli who?
Alligator, that's who.

KNOCK KNOCK!
Who's there?
Dawn.
Dawn who?
Dawn leave me out here in the cold.

KNOCK KNOCK!
Who's there?
You.
You who?
Did you call?

KNOCK KNOCK!
Who's there?
Pajamas.
Pajamas who?
Pajamas around me and hold me tight.

KNOCK KNOCK!
Who's there?
Sarah.
Sarah who?
Sarah doctor in the house?

KNOCK KNOCK!
Who's there?
Dishes.
Dishes who?
Dishes a very bad joke.

KNOCK KNOCK!
Who's there?
Oslo.
Oslo who?
Oslo down, what's the hurry?

KNOCK KNOCK!
Who's there?
Watson.
Watson who?
Watson television?

KNOCK KNOCK!
Who's there?
Says.
Says who?
Says me, that's who!

KNOCK KNOCK!
Who's there?
Aladdin.
Aladdin who?
Aladdin the street wants a word with you.

KNOCK KNOCK!
Who's there?
Amy.
Amy who?
Amy fraid I've forgotten.

KNOCK KNOCK!
Who's there?
Eddie.
Eddie who?
Eddie body home?

KNOCK KNOCK!
Who's there?
Beezer.
Beezer who?
Beezer black and yellow.

KNOCK KNOCK!
Who's there?
Heaven.
Heaven who?
Heaven seen you for ages.

KNOCK KNOCK!
Who's there?
Sacha.
Sacha who?
Sacha fuss, just because
I knocked at your door...

KNOCK KNOCK!
Who's there?
Fozzie.
Fozzie who?
Fozzie hundredth time, let me in!

KNOCK KNOCK!
Who's there?
Howie.
Howie who?
I'm fine, how are you?

KNOCK KNOCK!
Who's there?
Shirley.
Shirley who?
Shirley you must know me by now.

KNOCK KNOCK!
Who's there?
Adair.
Adair who?
Adair once but now I'm bald.

KNOCK KNOCK!
Who's there?
Witches.
Witches who?
Witches the way to go home?

KNOCK KNOCK!
Who's there?
Dummy.
Dummy who?
Dummy a favor and get lost.

Other titles in the *Sidesplitters* series you might enjoy:

0-7534-5708-3

0-7534-5725-3

0-7534-5706-7

0-7534-5709-1